SIDELINED FOR CHARACTER BUILDING

"But they that wait upon the LORD shall renew their strength; they shall mount up with wings as eagles; they shall run, and not be weary; and they shall walk, and not faint."
Isaiah 40:31 King James Version (KJV)

By

Ricky Martin

TABLE OF CONTENTS

Acknowledgment... 1

Letter to GOD 2

Introduction.. 3

Chapter 1: Stewardship: GOD is First 6

Chapter 2: Intimacy with GOD: How Prayer Prepares You.. 18

Chapter 3: Confessing the WORD: Renewing the Mind 24

Chapter 4: Ministry: Are You Ready? 37

Chapter 5: The Call of Leadership 49

TABLE OF CONTENTS

Acknowledgment 1

Letter to GOD 2

Introduction 3

Chapter 1: Stewardship: GOD is First 6

Chapter 2: Intimacy with GOD: How Prayer Prepares You .. 18

Chapter 3: Confessing the WORD: Renewing the Mind 24

Chapter 4: Ministry: Are You Ready? 37

Chapter 5: The Call of Leadership 49

ACKNOWLEDGMENT AND THANKS

First, I'd like to thank my wife, Nakeba. Without you, this would not have been possible. Our love continues to grow. "Living for the love of you!"

And to my kids, Ricquez, Jazara, and Tabre. If you believe it, you will achieve it.

In addition, I'd like to thank my mentors: Della Shelgren, Bishop EL Dillard, Pastor Lawrence Manson, Overseer Helen Seenster, Pastor Charles Walker, Overseer Tammy Harris, and Apostle Diane Brazil. Thank you for the countless hours mentoring me!

To my family and friends, I love you!

To my church family, From Broken to Healed Ministries,

I love you!

"Warrior Nation, Stand Up."

Father, I thank you for giving me the grace to start and finish this project. Without you, I am nothing. For 39 years you have been training and developing me for this moment. You are and forever will be my heart's desire.

Love, Ricky

Dear Reader,

I pray that the power of these words from my heart flow to your heart. May the words of this book be a **_stick of dynamite_** for you. May the words of this book penetrate your heart, destroy mindsets, and cultivate your character.

Sincerely,
Ricky

INTRODUCTION

"WHEN THE STUDENT IS READY, THE TEACHER APPEARS."

James 1:2-4 Amplified Bible (AMP)

"Consider it nothing but joy, my brothers and sisters, whenever you fall into various trials. Be assured that the testing of your faith [through experience] produces endurance [leading to spiritual maturity, and inner peace]. [4]

And let endurance have its perfect result and do a thorough work, so that you may be perfect and completely developed [in your faith], lacking in nothing."

In college football, millions of dollars are spent on scouting, football support staff, and recruitment. A report highlighting Georgia athletics issued in March 2020 stated that the football program spent $3.7 million on recruitment alone during the 2019 fiscal year.

Do Georgians love football? Yes, and they probably take their scouting and recruitment process with profound seriousness.

With that, imagine spending millions of dollars for one football recruit who has the potential to take the football program to the next level, only to discover that he has extensive off-the-field development issues.

Knowing the trickle-down effect of a losing season would bring about much turmoil with the athletic director, donors, and alumni, but this coach does not just think of today; he is pursuing tomorrow. He thinks to himself: "How can I get this young man's attention? What measures do I need to take to get this young man to care about his life off the field?"

"This young man has all the talent and no discipline. What can I do?" As the coach ponders his decision, he says to himself, "I've got it. I know what needs to be done. I will sideline him and force him to watch the game he loves from the bench. I will use his frustration of not playing and being sidelined as a catalyst to provoke motivation." The coach smiles to himself as the young man stands next to him watching the game.

Do I need to tell you the rest? The coach got the young man's attention. Why? Because being sidelined has a way of getting us to pay attention when we do not want to listen. Patience will have its perfect work, whether we like it or not.

James 1:4 (NIV) tells us to let perseverance *(tenacity, resolve, diligence, patience, purposefulness)* finish its work so that you may be mature and complete, not lacking (*wanting, deficient, inadequate, flawed*) anything.

Sometimes in life it feels like everyone else is moving ahead but you. You are in a race and everyone is running past you. You're ready to play the game, but you've been sidelined. It seems like GOD is blessing everyone, but you. You question GOD, "Why not me, LORD?"

Have you pondered on the thought that maybe GOD cares more about your character resume than your talent or your gift? He is the coach and he decided to sideline you with the intent of getting your attention.

GOD wants His glory to be revealed in you. If you study the word "glory" in Hebrew it's *kabad*. According to Strong's 3519b it means: glorious, honor, splendor, wealth, riches, honorable, bosom and soul to be heavy, weighty, or burdensome. When it says the GLORY of GOD, it means HIS nature, the full weight of His character. GOD wants HIS character, HIS nature, HIS glory to be revealed in us and manifested through us.

But can you handle being sidelined?

> *"…but we also glory in our sufferings, because we know that suffering produces perseverance; perseverance, character; and character, hope* (Romans 5:3).

CHAPTER 1

STEWARDSHIP: GOD IS FIRST

Matthew 25:14-30 English
Standard Version (ESV)

THE PARABLE OF THE TALENTS

"For it will be like a man going on a journey, who called his servants and entrusted to them his property. To one he gave five talents, to another two, to another one, to each according to his ability. Then he went away. He who had received the five talents went at once and traded with them, and he made five talents more. So also, he who had the two talents made two talents more. But he who had received the one talent went and dug in the ground and hid his master's money. Now after a long time the master of those servants came and settled accounts with them. And he who had received the five talents came forward, bringing five talents more, saying, 'Master, you delivered to me five talents; here, I have made five talents more.' His master said to him, 'Well done, good and faithful servant. You have been faithful over a little; I will set you over much. Enter into

the joy of your master.' And he also who had the two talents came forward, saying, 'Master, you delivered to me two talents; here, I have made two talents more.' His master said to him, 'Well done, good and faithful servant. You have been faithful over a little; I will set you over much. Enter into the joy of your master.' He also who had received the one talent came forward, saying, 'Master, I knew you to be a hard man, reaping where you did not sow, and gathering where you scattered no seed, so I was afraid, and I went and hid your talent in the ground. Here, you have what is yours.' But his master answered him, 'You wicked and slothful servant! You knew that I reap where I have not sown and gather where I scattered no seed? Then you ought to have invested my money with the bankers, and at my coming I should have received what was my own with interest. So take the talent from him and give it to him who has the ten talents. For to everyone who has will more be given, and he will have an abundance. But from the one who has not, even what he has will be taken away. And cast the worthless servant into the outer darkness. In that place there will be weeping and gnashing of teeth.'"

MANAGEMENT

The title of my first sermon was, "Are You a Steward of Your Time, Talent, and Money?" I had no idea that GOD was introducing me to stewardship. Stewardship is not always taught in the body of Christ and we treat it as if it is the last quality that we should develop, when in TRUTH it is the FIRST.

In this parable, Jesus is dealing with many topics, but one in particular resonates with me, and that is management. I know many gifted individuals in the body of Christ who are great teachers, preachers, and musicians who have not developed management skills. As we Pentecostals say, "They flow in the anointing." Yes, they flow in the anointing, but they are not good stewards.

I love the definition of management by Dr. Myles Munroe, who says proper management is the CORRECT use of something. To use something correctly implies that we will use it with integrity, including your time, money, and talent.

During my younger years, I thought it was a blessing that GOD paid my bills. As I grew in the LORD, I had to change my thinking. Now I say things like: "LORD, teach me how to manage what I have," or, "LORD, teach me how to budget the finances I oversee." It was not a blessing for GOD to pay my bills because I mismanaged the finances He gave me to pay my bills. I thank GOD for grace and mercy!

I remember buying a $16,000 car when my salary was only $21,000. Just because the bank approves you, does not mean you can afford it. Was I an impulse buyer? Most definitely—guilty—case closed.

The great Bishop E.L. Dillard once said: "We stumble over simplicity. Ricky, we stumble." Yes, we indeed stumble on the simple things in life. We seem to think that being practical is not spiritual.

In this chapter we will discuss **diligence**, **discipline,** and **routine.** All three are practical and simple, but immensely powerful. When we develop and implement them, they will produce an amazing harvest. Let us explore them.

DILIGENCE

In Genesis 1:26 GOD says, *"Let us make man in our image and likeness and let them have dominion!"* GOD had always intended for Adam to manage what He created. Understanding this truth, we come to the knowledge that we do not owe anything. We are tasked only to oversee; to be stewards over what was given to us to manage. Psalm 115:16 says, *"The heaven, even the heavens, are the LORD's: but the earth **hath he given** to the children of men."*

Diligence means "**careful and persistent work or effort**." Being diligent means that you are tenacious with every goal, in every project, and with every endeavor. Another way to say it: You maximize the minimum. You take the little bit you were given and maximize it to its fullest potential.

Are you tired of starting something only to stop just a few weeks later? How many projects have you started? How many dreams have you invested in, only to stop after the newness of the hype wore off? How many times have you started and because of unseen changes in your plan, you stopped?

Diligence also means to press forward despite changes, setbacks, hinderances, and what I like to call the "stuff in between." Can you hold on to a dream for years without seeing it manifest? Do you have the strength to hold on to dreams and manage disappointments?

I was young **and overly ambitious**, full of vision, but I lacked diligence. I had no problem dreaming, seeing visions, and speaking faith into existence. I could stand on the WORD, but little did I know standing without resistance is easy but standing WITH resistance is different.

Standing with resistance taught me two things: (1) How much I procrastinate; and (2) Disappointment is a blessing.

GOD has a way of pushing you toward perfection. I struggled with procrastination. It would take me forever just to do a simple task.

I had a major problem with following through and staying on task. Truth be told, I was lazy! To be successful, you need to be honest with yourself, if not, then be prepared to be on the sideline because your character is not ready.

THE DANGER OF PROCRASTINATION

A diligent person is persistent, putting up a constant effort at every corner and pushing through times of uncertainty and adversity. The enemy of diligence is procrastination. Procrastination is a silent killer. It's "the canker worm" that will eat away dreams, visions, and hopes. Procrastination is putting or delaying or postponing something. Many individuals struggle with completing projects. I have learned the best way to combat procrastination is to start small. Do not try to complete a huge project in one setting. Preparation is 90% of the battle. Take it from someone who struggled with procrastination for many years.

I struggled because my mind was overwhelmed with the many stages or steps needed to complete a project. Often, I would skip steps because I wanted to finish. When the task or project was finally done, it was sloppy and not my best work. Luke 14:28 says, *"For which of you, desiring to build a tower, does not first sit down and count the cost, whether he has enough to complete it."* **Little by little** will be your secret power to overcoming procrastination. Set up small tasks for yourself and you will see astonishing results. Charles Spurgeon has an amazing quote: "By ***perseverance*** the snail reached the ark."

Remember: Nothing that has value will be obtained easily!

DISCIPLINE

The word *discipline* means **"to train"** or **"is developed by instructions and exercised by self-control."**

Without discipline you will not succeed and you will not persevere. Discipline is making intentional decisions to keep oneself on the path of purpose.

In Matthew 25:14-15, each servant was given stewardship over the talents provided to them according to their own ability. (Enduring Word)

This was not a strange idea in the ancient world, where servants were often given great responsibility. This was not unconventional; it was the safest thing a man could do with his money. The talent was not a coin. It was a weight and therefore its value obviously depended on whether the coinage involved was copper, gold, or silver (Barclay). In the application of this parable, it is appropriate to see these **talents** as life resources, such as time, money, abilities, and authority.

The servants were given different amounts of money according to their ability. One servant received one talent, yet we should see that this was not an insignificant amount. Some received more; but everyone received something, and everyone received a large amount. (Enduring Word)

The talent each man has suits his own state best; and it is only pride and insanity which would lead him (or any of us) to desire and envy the graces and talents of another. Five talents would be too much for some men; one talent would be too little. (Clarke)

The servants were tasked with managing the master's money. Each of those who had received talents from their master did with them as they saw fit.

Two of them traded with their talents and earned more talents (made another five talents… gained two more, as well).

They **went and traded** implies direct action. It implies discipline; the servants made intentional decisions!

The point is that the good servants felt the responsibility of their assignment and went to work without delay. (Carson)

We are not told how they **traded with** their talents. Perhaps they loaned the money at interest; perhaps they used the money and bought things and sold them for more money.

The point is that they used what they had and gained more by doing so. (Enduring Word)

We can say many good things about the work of the first two servants:

- They did their work promptly.
- They did their work with perseverance.
- They did their work with success.
- They were disciplined.
- They were intentional.
- They were diligent.
- They were ready to give an account to their master.

The two good and faithful servants give us an example of stewardship at its best. Because they were disciplined and made intentional decisions, they were given MORE authority and rulership over what the master owned.

The third servant did almost nothing with his master's money. He took some care that it would not be lost (by hiding it), but he did nothing productive with his master's money, in contrast to the first two servants.

The principle of this parable is stewardship. Jesus is revealing that WE as servants do not OWN anything and everything belongs to the Father (the master).

What belongs to the Father? Everything! Our money, our careers, our marriage decisions, our business decisions, how we spend money, and even where we live. The list goes on and on; it all belongs to HIM. We do not own anything but are only overseeing according to our ability.

Allow me to let you in on a secret...If YOU are crucified with HIM… Hello…you no longer live, but the LIFE you now live is according to the FAITH of the SON of Man who loves you and gave Himself for you.

Pause and take a moment to soak in and digest what you just read. It is not about how much you know or how much information you absorb if you cannot apply what was revealed.

Hint: That is what I call head knowledge vs. heart knowledge. Head knowledge is knowing and quoting scripture. Head knowledge does not even require a relationship with Christ! Why? Because it is in your head!

Heart knowledge is different. It's applying scripture to your daily life with an open communion with the Holy Spirit. When the WORD is in your heart, it develops a relationship with GOD that is deeper and wider than a person who "knows" scriptures.

What is the third servant's excuse? *"LORD, I knew you to be a hard man, reaping where you have not sown, and gathering where you have not scattered seed. And I was afraid and went and hid your talent in the ground."* Matthew 25-24-30

We can say of the third servant: He did not think, he did not work, he did not even try, and he made excuses. He was not disciplined!

Notice in the parable the master said, "You wicked and lazy servant," (Matthew 25:26-30) but not in the traditional vocabulary we are used to. Usually we hear wickedness and we instantly think of sinful characteristics. We seldom associate wickedness with laziness and mismanagement.

He operated in wickedness because he was lazy, fearful, and undisciplined. Can we say that we sin and walk in wickedness when we mismanage our marriages, jobs, churches, ministries, and finances?

GOD has given us grace, but are we operating? Do you evangelize, do you pray for the sick, do you give unto the LORD?

The charge against this third servant who merely buried his talent was that he was wicked, lazy, and undisciplined. Rarely is laziness seen as a real sin, something that must be repented of before the LORD. If laziness were a calling or a spiritual gift, this man would have been excellent. (Enduring Word)

Discipline helps you stay on track and prevents mismanagement. Myles Munroe said it best: "What you manage you will attract. It will be drawn to you, but what you mismanage you will lose."

ROUTINE

What attributes do a disciplined man or woman have in common? A routine. A routine is a sequence of actions that are regularly followed, a fixed program. Having a disciplined routine is what binds everything together and without it projects are left incomplete. The two servants probably had a routine: they woke up early, checked the market, analyzed trends, and conducted trades.

If your focus is to maximize what has been given to you, a disciplined routine will help you maximize the return. This includes marriage, ministry, career, and everything that you oversee.

A disciplined man prays diligently and consistently seeks direction for his family. A disciplined pastor repeatedly seeks out strategies from the LORD for the direction of the ministry and will not move until the LORD speaks.

A disciplined mother is a virtuous woman (Proverbs 31). *"She rises while it is still night and gives meat to her household. She is like the merchant ships and brings her food from afar. A mother, a virtuous women's child, will arise up and call her blessed."*

A routine does not mean your life is boring It means that you are diligent, and you desire to maximize what you have been given.

Please do not misunderstand me, no matter how driven you are, breaks, vacations, family time, and date nights are important as well. They serve as a refresher to help us focus on first things first.

Prioritizing is knowing what is first and who is first. GOD honors our relationships and watches closely to see how we value them. Fathers, mothers, leaders, and pastors: please do not sacrifice your family on the altar of success. A ministry, a church, or your career is not more important than your family.

I believe GOD is calling The Body of Christ to acknowledge and come into the understanding of true stewardship and the weight that it carries.

CHAPTER 2

INTIMACY WITH GOD: HOW PRAYER PREPARES YOU

"He that dwelleth in the secret place of the most High shall abide under the shadow of the Almighty." Psalm 91:1

I have seen GOD do many wonders in my life through prayer. There are many books on prayer and how to seek His presence. Prayer was not intended to be complex; prayer is closeness. Prayer is simple; it is not about time. It is not about how long you pray or using the right words when you pray; it is about consistency.

Most people think their prayers are not answered because of how they pray. The Bible says that when you pray, you must believe that you have received, believing that you have received is the requirement. It is not about using the right words or knowing the exact methods. Prayer is built on love and carried by faith. You do not have to know everything about prayer to see results. Only faith is required for results to be achieved. If someone told you that you need to know the five secret steps to receive in prayer, do not believe the indoctrination.

Believers second-guess themselves when it correlates to "steps." Did I do it right? Did I forget a step? Is it the right order? Will my prayers be heard? Does GOD even hear me? Prayer is where the WORD processes the "thing" in your heart. Hebrews 4:12 (ESV) says, *"For the word of GOD is living and active, sharper than any two-edge sword, piercing to the divisions of the soul* **(mind)** *and spirit* **(heart), of joints and of marrow, and discerning the thoughts and intentions of the heart."**

The word of GOD powered by the Holy Spirit will penetrate the mind (*soul realm*) and heart with the anointing to destroy (*demolish, never to rise again*) strongholds of wrong thinking and wrong believing. It is a heart walk. Prayer gives the Holy Spirit a full examination of the intents and motivations of the heart. I know what you are thinking: "Do I need a prayer life to function in ministry?" The answer is NO. Shocking, right? You can do ministry without a prayer life. You can pastor a church, preach, heal the sick, cast out demons. It does not require a prayer life, but faith.

"Wait—what did you say?"

How do I know this? Because it was me. I operated for years in ministry without an established prayer life and many across the world are in the same ship. What I am talking about is, before and after you minister, does your prayer life match what you demonstrated?

As I said in the introduction, GOD cares more about your character than He does your ministry.

Enough of that. We'll cover this more in the next few chapters.

What is this secret place?

HE THAT DWELLETH

The Hebrew word for "dwell" is *Yashab,* which means **"to sit down, to dwell, to remain, to sit, to abide, to be inhabited."** He that dwelleth is the one who habitually remains in the secret place. They are the ones who have made the secret place their "home." The problem with many believers today is inconsistency. Is there a place or a store you always visit? The moment you walk in, you know exactly where everything is, and you even know if the store rearranged where certain items used to be. To top that, the staff knows you and most likely the owner does, too. Why? Because you habitually shop there; you are a consistent shopper.

Why can't we be like that with our Father's presence? We need to be! Jesus says in John 14:23, *"If a man loves me, he will keep my words: and my Father will love him, and we will come unto him, and make our abode with him."* Let me clarify, GOD's presence is always with us! He will never leave us nor will he forsake us: GOD is love and He loves us unconditionally and He will never stop. Believe it or not, all believers are called to prayer, but only a few accept and carry the call of prayer.

To answer the call and carry the burden has one specific essential. The assignment is to dwell, to habitually visit the secret place of The Most High under all circumstances.

THE SECRET PLACE OF THE MOST HIGH

Let me first establish this distinction: The secret place is not a secret. Jesus says in Matthew 6:6 (ESV): *"But when you pray, go into **your room**, and **shut the door** and pray to your Father **who is in secret**. And your Father who **sees in secret** will reward you."*

The word "secret" used in Matthew 6:6 is *Kryptos,* meaning **"hidden, concealed, secret, private."** When Jesus said to "go into your room," the specific word "room" was used for a storeroom where treasures were kept.

He does not want us to be like hypocrites. In early Greek culture, the hypocrites referenced actors who played roles. Those individuals would see the world as their stage to perform and set out to put on a good show. Jesus wants us to do the opposite: do not perform for the audience; do not put on a public display to attract attention. Do not use mystic, hollow words and pointless echoes. Instead, let it flow from the heart. The Bible says that the prayer of the righteous person has power as it is working (James 5:16). Your prayers prevail and are effective because of your faith and righteousness *(your position in Christ)* not because of big words or even a systemic process.

In Psalm 91, the word "secret" is *cether,* meaning, **"covering, shelter, hiding place, secrecy, secret place."** The Psalm is referring to a designated physical place of refuge. In the movie *War Room*, we see Psalm 91 and Matthew 6 unite. The Miss Clara character played by Karen Abercrombie illustrates an awesome demonstration. She created a special closet where she decided to pray and war against the enemy. I love the scene in which the retired pastor and his wife are thinking of purchasing Miss Clara's home and he walks into what used to be her war room and paces back and forth before saying to the realtor, "Somebody has been praying in here; it is like it's baked in!"

It was a designated physical space where Miss Clara secretly sought closeness with the Father and did warfare. As Bishop Paul Morton stated, warfare is spirit over the mind. You must allow The Word of GOD to be placed in the highest seat of the soul. This is done in prayer and over periods of time. Remember, I am not talking about the ability to do ministry, which can be done without a prayer life. This is about **your** relationship with GOD!

Do you have to have a designated space? No. Is that the only place where warfare is done, in the prayer room? No. You can pray anywhere, and do warfare everywhere, but let it come from the heart. If you feel like GOD is prompting you to create a designated space, then act upon it and do it swiftly.

Shall Abide "Under the Shadow of the Almighty"

His promise is straightforward to the one who habitually "dwells" in the secret physical designated "room" or shelter of GOD shall *(a promised word)* abide *(lodge, remain)* under the shadow *(cover, protection)* of the Almighty.

The shadow of the Almighty is an expression that implies great nearness. We must walk remarkably close to a companion, if we would have his shadow fall on us. (Duncan, cited in Spurgeon)

I once illustrated this at church during Bible study. I asked one of the pastors to stand with his arms stretched out like the Christ the Redeemer statue in Rio De Janeiro and I went and lay at his feet. The illustration was to show everyone what it meant to lie at the feet of Jesus.

Now think of this: If I am lying at His feet, then his shadow is covering me, which makes it hard to attack me. Why? Because before the things attack me, they must first come through His shadow!

Therefore, whatever attacks me GOD has permitted and has empowered me to walk through anything that comes my way. (Romans 8:37; 1 Corinthians 10:13; and 2 Corinthians 2:13-15)

Make it your pursuit to habitually dwell in HIS presence under HIS shadow.

CHAPTER 3

CONFESSING THE WORD: RENEWING THE MIND

Romans 12:2 English Standard Version (ESV)

"Do not be conformed to this world,[a] but be transformed by the renewal of your mind, that by testing you may discern what is the will of GOD, what is good and acceptable and perfect."

Many believers struggle with The will of GOD. We want to know what our purpose is. We ask the questions: "Why was I created? What is GOD's plan for me? What is acceptable? How do I deepen my relationship with GOD?" It all starts with renewing our minds.

Renewing the mind requires that we not be hearers only, but doers. The reason why many do not renew their minds is because they fail to apply what they hear. If you only hear and do not change your thinking, then you are not being renewed. You will be saved by grace but will live like a heathen.

Mind renewal is my favorite topic to teach and preach. The process of renewing the mind will challenge you. It will push you to confront hidden patterns of incorrect thinking that are buried in acceptance and rationale.

Sin loves to hide behind acceptance and rationale. Sin knows that in order to keep operating, it must deceive the user into rationalizing and denial. For sin's plan to work, it must hide deep behind the strongholds of wrong thinking. These strongholds are built over time and are heavily guarded by demonic thinking patterns. The strongman of wrong thinking is the spirit of perversion. Perversion is believing something is right when it's wrong. It is taking truth and bending it to fit your perception.

Renewing your mind is the WORD of GOD breaking and destroying your perception that is guarded by demonic thinking. Just like Joshua and the walls of Jericho, the WORD destroys the walls never to rise again.

"Is not my word like fire, declares the LORD, ***and like a hammer that breaks the rock in pieces?"*** (Jeremiah 23:29)

"Therefore, put away all filthiness and rampant wickedness and ***receive with meekness the implanted word, which is able to save your souls.*** *"* (James 1:21)

Get ready to dive deep into the renewing process and I promise you that your life will never be the same.

STRONGHOLDS

A physical stronghold is a **fortified wall** used to protect oneself against attacks. The **wall** is considered a stronghold and is heavily manned by military armed forces. **The wall** is used as a defensive strategy **to give those behind it** the higher ground.

In nearly all occasions the armed forces defending the wall are outnumbered by the pursuing army. The objectives of the military behind the wall are (1) Use the wall to their advantage; (2) Let nothing in; (3) Let nothing out; and (4) At all cost stand and defend the wall.

Mental strongholds are the same; **the fortified wall** in our minds is built by traumatic occurrences. Trauma, if permitted, will build a stronghold mentally. When trauma builds, it uses past experiences as gatekeepers, allowing nothing in or out to keep the mindset safe.

The mindset operates behind the walls and its job is to control individuals while staying undetected. Many people display behaviors with a lack of understanding of why they behave or react to certain situations. The mindset created by trauma wants the individual to believe what they experience or have is their reality.

Not all mindsets are created by trauma; any mindset can be learned by observation. For example, many children learn mindsets by watching their parents' behavior. Generational curses are taught that spirits pass down from one generation to the next and in order to break them we must cast the demon out.

True, however I argue this point: if you cast the demon out but the mindset still exists, will the demon return? Yes, because casting out a demon and not renewing the mind is a temporary remedy.

However, if you renew the mind, it will destroy the fortified wall and unseat the demonic authority in power. The demonic authority in power could be a demonic presence or sinful reality.

Strongholds are built brick by brick, so do not get offended when your structure is not assembled to your fancy. Renewing the mind is an indication of true discipleship.

HOW DO YOU RENEW THE MIND?

To understand what mind renewal is, I must establish the truth at salvation. Romans 10:9 says, *"If you confess with your mouth that Jesus is LORD and believe in your heart that GOD raised him from the dead, you will be saved."* You are saved, but at that moment your mind has not been delivered. Your memories are not erased, the pain and hurt you endured exist; the trauma exists, the abuse, the molestation is over, but still very real in your consciousness.

Colossians 3:1-5 says, *"If then you have been raised with Christ, seek the things that are above, where Christ is, seated at the right hand of*

GOD. *Set your minds on things that are above*, *not on things that are on earth. For you have died, and your life is hidden with Christ in GOD. When Christ who is your[a] life appears, then you also will appear with him in glory.*

Put to death therefore what is earthly in you."

Because sin starts in the mind, it needs to be cleansed from the inside out. Curry Blake's *Mind Renewal Manual* states: **"Mind renewal is the restoration of the mental faculties** of a Christian to the state that GOD originally intended man to operate in. **Mind renewal is renovating the mind of a Christian.** It is the **removal** of information, patterns, mindsets, attitudes, and limitations that would not be found in the Mind of Christ."

> *"And be not conformed to this world: but be ye transformed*
> *by the renewing of your mind, that ye may prove what is that*
> *good, and acceptable, and perfect will of GOD"*
> (Romans 12:2 KJV).

The renewing of the Christian's mind is its restoration into a state of continuous harmony and synchronization with the Mind of Christ. It is simply "reprogramming" a Christian's carnal (fallen state) mind to function and operate in the same manner and with the same efficiency as the Mind of Christ.

NOTICE! The only way we are told that our life will be changed is by the renewing of our mind. It does not say that we will be transformed by a prayer, a prophecy, having hands laid upon us, or any other method! It actually goes on to say that without having our mind renewed, we cannot prove the will of GOD.

We must decide and then follow through with the process of having our minds renovated.

That is why it is crucial to watch what we say! Matthew 12:34 says, *"For out the abundance of the heart the mouth speaks;"* Matthew 12:37 goes on to say: *"For by YOUR WORDS you will be justified (be made free or acquitted), and by YOUR WORDS you will be condemned (put in bondage or to be sentenced)."*

The key element to renewal is purely confession, declaring, and applying THE WORD OF GOD over your life. If you think about it, people are kept in bondage by the words they play and repeat in their minds.

Individuals are held in bondage by traumatic experiences because the event replays, rewinds, replays, rewinds, replays, rewinds, not knowing that each replay and rewind is building a structure brick by brick, creating a stronghold.

What we need to do as believers is declare the WORD of GOD in retaliation of the replay and rewind until its structure is no longer standing.

2 Corinthians 10:3-5 says, *"For though we walk in the flesh,* ***we do not war after the flesh:***

(For the weapons of our warfare are not carnal, but mighty through GOD to the pulling down of strong holds;)

Casting down imaginations, and every high thing that exalteth itself against the knowledge of GOD, and bringing into captivity every thought to the obedience of Christ."

The original Greek states "to **demolish the stronghold never to rise again."**

We cast down *(reject, block)* vain *(sinful)* imaginations *(images, pictures, or words)* that try to assert, exalt, or present themselves as truth. We seize hold of every image, picture, or word and forcefully bring it to the mirror of Christ's WORDS and HIS image. And if the picture or words do not match HIS image or HIS words, then cast it down and condemn it. This is what happens when we renew the mind.

Because we confessed the WORD, the Holy Spirit uses the WORD of GOD as the pursuing army to demolish, disarm, and unseat the image, picture, or words that are in authority and sets up a new King! The new King whose name is Jesus The Christ sits on the throne of your mind and manifests Himself from the inside out!

From Colossians 2:9-15: *"For in him the whole fullness of deity dwells bodily, and you have been filled in him, who is the head of all rule and authority. In him also you were circumcised with a circumcision made without hands, by putting off the body of the flesh, by the circumcision of Christ, having been buried with him in baptism, in which you were also raised with him through faith in the powerful working of GOD, who raised him from the dead.*

And you, who were dead in your trespasses and the uncircumcision of your flesh, GOD made alive together with him, having forgiven us all our

trespasses, **by canceling the record of debt that stood against us with its legal demands. This he set aside, nailing it to the cross. He disarmed the rulers and authorities and put them to open shame, by triumphing over them in him."**

CONFESSIONS

Have you ever wondered: How do I create a new mindset? Confession is done all the time. How? The Bible says out of the abundance of the heart the mouth speaks, right! Well, where does the abundance come from?

By now you should be aware of the fact that your mouth and your heart have a connection. What is in the heart comes or flows out of the mouth.

These traumatic experiences in our lives become stamped on the table of our hearts. What is in the heart becomes the creator of the stronghold; it is the strongman everyone is protecting. The heart is protected by the story we tell ourselves. What story are you telling yourself? What story has your heart told your mind to protect?

Being a victim of sexual abuse at the age of eight stamped a few things on my heart. It stamped intimacy issues; I did not like to be touched. It stamped low self-esteem and it stamped sexual perversion. What is stamped on the heart will create the how we behave.

The heart is the key! Proverbs 4:23 says, *"Above all else guard your heart, for everything you do flows from it."*

Confessing is declaring what GOD's word says. By confessing we are reprogramming the heart, removing the stench, and establishing a new way of thinking. Jesus's first message was repent, for the Kingdom of GOD is at hand. The word "repent" means to CHANGE the way you think! He was preaching mind renewal!

The Word of GOD is the Mind of GOD. By declaring what the Word says, we program our heart to receive the mind of GOD. Confession must be done daily. When Paul said, "I die daily," he was referring to putting to death his old nature, the old nature that resides in the mind. When we confess the WORD of GOD, it will be engrafted within our hearts and whatever is in the heart will produce a new thought pattern that will CHANGE our behavior. This is called Godly Strongholds.

GODLY STRONGHOLDS

In her book, *Switch On Your Brain*, Caroline Leaf says, "What you are thinking every moment of every day becomes a physical reality in your brain and body, which affects your optimal mental and physical health. These thoughts collectively form your attitude, which is your state of mind, and it's your attitude and not your DNA that determines much of the quality of life."

The real meaning: What you think becomes or is your physical reality. Believe it or not, you are a walking prophecy designed not by DNA but by the WORDS spoken to you and over you that were incubated throughout your life.

Creating Godly thinking patterns will build strongholds founded on the WORD of GOD. Let us build some **Godly Strongholds!**

Rejection

I come against you, rejection, and I speak over my life that I am accepted by GOD; I am **accepted** by HIM. I declare I will no longer allow myself to be offended, or victimized, by the opinions, actions, or words of people! I stand on the WORD of GOD, and I declare today, I am free!

Fear

Hello fear, it is me! And I am running toward you full speed, for GOD has not given me a spirit of fear, but of power, love, and a sound mind. I declare over myself that I am strong in the LORD. I declare, by the power of the Holy Spirit, I am courageous. I walk in power; I walk in love!

Anger

It is okay for me to be angry; it is okay for me to be upset. I have that right, but it is not okay for me to use my anger as an excuse to sin, to manipulate people, or to intimidate people. I will communicate in a mature way, for it is not my only language.

Emptiness/Loneliness

I am not alone. I am not alone. I am not alone. I am not alone. My God is with me. I reject and block my past emotional ties that created loneliness. I am filled with the Holy Spirit and I am never alone!

Depression

I will, I will, I will, I will, I will, lift UP my eyes unto the Hills. My help, my rescuer, my redeemer, my protector, my champion who made heaven and earth, will not allow my foot to be moved, for he never sleeps. For the LORD is in His Holy Temple (that is me). Let all the earth be silent!

Perversion

I will walk in truth. I will walk in justice. I will not lie. I will not pervert GOD's word to suit my opinion. I will walk in integrity. I will walk in full transparency!

Pride

GOD will resist me when I walk proudly in my own strength and in my own ability. But when I humble myself, He gives me grace. When I humble myself, GOD will exalt me.

I declare I am the righteousness GOD; I am in right standing with GOD; not by my works, but because of my Faith in Jesus The Christ.

DO YOU SEE ANYTHING?

Eighteen years ago, the church I attended was invited to sing in St. Paul, Minnesota. I had only been preaching for a year and my wife was pregnant with our son, Ricquez. After the choir sang and rejoiced, pastor Ann Waters started to teach. Little did I know her message would be embedded in my soul. Her topic was, "Do You See Anything?"

Many times in life we focus on accomplishing and making BIG changes, when in truth it's the SMALL ones that are missed. Ann's message helped me to focus on making small changes and being PROUD of what seemed like insignificant accomplishments, but were **huge!**

We have the inclination that small goals are meaningless. In fact, they are the opposite. I remember I wanted to be constant in prayer, so every day I committed myself to prayer for one minute. Really? Yes, I did. And from that one minute I grew by leaps and bounds. Remember, prayer is not about time, but consistency.

Do you see anything? What can you accomplish right now? What is a quick win for you? Do you see it?

The process of writing this book was done paragraph by paragraph every day; a small amount of writing here and there. Right now, you are reading a book written by a man who does not have a college degree!

We have many rooms in our minds that need to be cleansed. Renewing the mind is not, and I repeat, it is not an **overnight**

process, but not an excuse to be idle. Please remember to have grace for those in renewing stages that you were in before.

A change has come. It may not be a big change, but do you see anything? If you do, even if the change is small, change is change! Applaud it!

Do you see anything?

CHAPTER 4

MINISTRY:
ARE YOU READY?

Romans 5:3-5 English Standard Version (ESV)

*"Not only that, but **we rejoice in our sufferings**,
knowing that **suffering produces endurance**, and
**endurance produces character, and character
produces hope**, and hope does not put us to shame,
because GOD's love has been poured into our hearts through
the Holy Spirit who has been given to us."*

I must advise you, reading this chapter will probably be offensive to the flesh. I encourage you to keep going. It may get ugly, but that is good! Why? Because change is not always wrapped up pretty with a bow under a tree.

A LONG KISS OF SUFFERINGS

The theme of this book is character development. But how does GOD develop character?

My first question to you is: Have you learned how to rejoice in the midst of pressure? The Greek word "sufferings" in Romans chapter 3 is *thlipsis,* which means: **"oppression, affliction, tribulation, distress, a pressing, pressing together, pressure."**

Paul is telling us GOD's methodology of developing character. First point: **Stop running**! Many of us have the propensity to run away while under fire, facing pressure, tribulation, stress, or affliction. Developing character means you run to the sound of battle! The Bible says that as Goliath moved closer to attack, David ran quickly to meet him. Now is the time for you to throw away your running shoes and stand firm footed.

Nothing is stronger than a made-up mind. When you decide and stand firm on that decision, nothing can shake it. Make up your mind that you will no longer run away because of fear, pressure, anxiety, and stress. I challenge you to express joy (*rejoice*), not for the stress, pressure, anxiety but knowing that the tribulation was permitted for the optimization of your character.

THE TANK ENGINE THAT COULD

Next in the development stage is endurance (Romans 5: *knowing that* **suffering produces endurance**). We know that suffering is **pressure, affliction, tribulation, distress, a pressing together** all designed to produce endurance. The

Biblical term for "endurance" is *patience or perseverance*. GOD has given you the strength to shoulder the weight of the pressure, oppression, tribulation, and affliction. For our muscles to grow they must first be torn; this is called hypertrophy. It is in this torn stage that the muscles are pushed to their limit.

Hypertrophy is achieved because the muscles suffer under intense pressure. This pressure is what builds the muscle. *"Godly suffering, Godly pressure builds endurance; And we know that for those who love GOD all things work together for good, for those who are called according to his purpose."* (Romans 8:28)

In the Bible there are a few instances where affliction was permitted by GOD for growth. In the first chapter of Exodus, a pharaoh arose who knew not Joseph and was afraid that the Israelites were too mighty and could overpower them if any had joined their enemy. So he commanded the taskmasters to oppress them, but the more they were afflicted, pressed, and made to carry burdens, the more they grew and multiplied.

In chapter 8 of Acts, the apostles were only preaching in smaller cities and the gospel had not spread out of Jerusalem, but when the church faced a great persecution, then they were scattered abroad. GOD had used oppression, tribulation, and affliction as a mechanism to push the gospel all over the regions.

GOD does not put sickness on us to teach us a lesson, but while we are battling and enduring that infirmity, we develop. In James 5, we are charged to lay hands on the sick and they shall recover, but it does not say how long that recovery timeframe is. The purpose of endurance is to refine you like gold and bring forth Godly character.

CHARACTER LIKE JOSEPH

When it comes to character, Joseph is one who stands out. What he suffered by the hands of his own family would have destroyed many people, but he endured and despite their act of betrayal his character never wavered. Romans 5: *endurance produces character!*

If pressure produces patience and patience produces character, then there is only one conclusion: Godly character is molded by fire. In Romans 5, the word "character" is *dokime*, which means **"proving trial, approved, tried character, an example tried worth."** Before character is proven, it must be tried by fire. In Revelation 3:18, GOD says, *"I counsel you to buy from me gold refined by fire."*

In his book, *The Fire of Delayed Answers*, Bob Sorge says that buying refined gold from GOD is a two-fold answer; the gold is purified faith and refined character.

John 15:2 says, *"Every branch in me that does not bear fruit he takes away, and every branch that does bear he prunes, that it may bear fruit."*

The Father's desire is that we bear fruit and if we abide *(persist)* in him *(fellowship)* we will bear much fruit. The fruit is the substance of Godly character. Fruit is what people see. Can it be seen in you? What is Godly character, love, joy, peace, patience, kindness, goodness, faithfulness, gentleness, and self-control? Are you bearing fruit? You have an awesome gift, but you are rude to people, you show up late, not respecting others' time. You preach well, but you are not faithful, you are impatient when listening to others, arrogance reeks from your presence, and you always have to be right.

You can believe it or choose to disregard it, but there is no way to go around it: character is produced when you have persevered in affliction, tribulation, pressure, stress, and anxiety. It is the pressure that measures the amount of WORD in you when you are in a trial. Go through, let GOD manifest His character in you, and it will transcend things around you.

THE ELPIS EFFECT

"...and character produces __hope__, and __hope__ does not put us to shame, because GOD's love has been poured into our hearts through the Holy Spirit who has been given to us." (Romans 5:3-5)

What is hope? Hope is **"tiqvah,"** which is defined as **"expectancy, expectation, expected, the thing that you have longed for, and a cord as an attachment."** Another word that describes hope is "elpis," which means **"to have a joyful and confident expectation of eternal salvation."** Elpis is the persuader of hope, to have hope, to live in hope, and to hope. Now picture in your mind seeing a large ship and a huge anchor being lowered into the depths of the water. The anchor's assignment is stopping the ship from moving, but without the rope (cord) the anchor is nonessential. Jesus is that anchor and our hope is the rope (the cord) that determines how deep the anchor holds.

I am tempted to ask you: Are you anchored in hope? Does your rope hang low? How is a rope made? The rope is composed of a group of yarn, plies, and fibers that are twisted together in a large and stronger form. Rope is equipped with tensile strength, meaning it can be used for dragging and lifting. The thicker the rope, the more it can hold. If the tribulations we encounter and press through produces yarn, then it is evident that the length and the strength of our hope is built on preserving faith. It is fire *(metaphorically fire by trials)* that binds the rope together strengthening our hope!

Hope, therefore, is seeing that you are being transformed into the image of Christ. Hope establishes the great exchange; where you lay down your life and pick up His life and become a living epistle and Christ is manifested for all to witness.

GOD has His plan and He will use our sufferings and the things we contend with to bring out the best in us. The Bible is precise. Only fire produces character, and that character will establish an everlasting hope!

"Blessed is the man who trusts in the Lord,

whose trust is the Lord.

He is like a tree planted by water,

that sends out its roots by the stream,

and does not fear when heat comes,

for its leaves remain green,

WHAT IS MINISTRY?

Before I could describe what ministry is, I had to define what should be the foundation of ministry. The substance of ministry is built on character and integrity. It is why you do what you do. Is it out of love or just for the accolades of people? I have witnessed many individuals do ministry for selfish gain. GOD has always put in me not to perform, but to let it flow from the heart. Ministry is simply meeting the needs of people. That is all ministry is. Ministry is fulfilling the great commission to go out into the world and preach, teach, make disciples, cast out devils, lay hands, and be clothed with love.

Mark 16:14-20 and Matthew 28:16-20 are both awesome foundational ministry directives to glean from. In Mark 16, Jesus appears to the disciples, who at the time are reclining. Strange; your leader is gone and you have time to relax? Jesus rebukes them for their disbelief and hardness of heart. He then tells them why: because after all this time they did not believe the others when they told them they saw Him. I imagine the disciples having sunken faces when they saw Jesus. Ashamed because their lack of belief was exposed, but like any great leader Jesus did not leave them wallowing in failure; instead he followed up with instructions to GO! And did they GO. He commanded them to preach to all creation, baptize those that believed, and said signs would follow them.

It is important to point out that the signs followed them because they believed first, not the other way around. If you believe first, then signs will follow. Here are the signs, casting out demons, speaking in tongues, laying hands on the sick, making disciples, and teaching. Simple. Then why do we make ministry so difficult and convoluted?

It is not complex. Whatever you do, do it with a pure heart. Ministry is "the work" of the Kingdom, but character is the "why" behind the work. Ministry has a great track record; it will expose you and though it may seem like you are getting away, it is just a matter of time. I love the phrase, "The wheels of justice turn slowly and exceedingly fine." My prayer to GOD was: "LORD, do not increase my influence in ministry if my character is not in line." Your gift will take you to the top, to the place of influence, but will the gift keep you saved? NO!

DHT AND THE TRUTH ABOUT THE ANOINTING

I was introduced to Divine Healing Technician (DHT) teaching in 2015 by my co-worker and friend Christine. Let me tell you the truth: this teaching by Curry Blake paradigm-shifted the delusion I had about the anointing. By the way, there were many sacred cows I cleaved to, but I want to discuss the truth of the anointing. I grew up Pentecost and was taught to believe that the more you pray the more anointed you became. I believed the more hours I spent in prayer the more anointed I would be when the time came for me to preach. I would typically spend six to eight hours the night before praying in tongues for GOD to move in the atmosphere when it was time for me to preach. This is not including the hours I spent seeking GOD for a word. I believed the more "I" did the more "HE" would use me. Are you starting to see a pattern? "I." I was relying on my ability to produce the anointing by praying, fasting. In my subconscious mind *(belief system),* I believed that the anointing of GOD could be increased if an individual worked hard enough. I know this sounds crazy, but it is what I believed.

The teaching you sit under will build a belief system and along the way you inherently pick up the mannerisms of the teacher. What I could not see was my belief system was not built on faith but on works. I had unintentionally walked away from Grace. I forgot about Jesus! Unbeknownst to me, I was operating in pride and often looked down on people who could not fast like I could or pray as I could. The mindset I created was: "Ricky" is anointed because I pray and read the word constantly. What is in the sky? It's a bird. No, it's a plane. NO, it was the DHT training manual that pulverized my mindset.

What eliminated the errors in my mindset was the acknowledgment and the truth of the atonement. I did not know that healing was included in the atonement. I had spent most of my life begging and pleading with GOD to heal and deliver from a position of "if" it is your will. Acts 10:38 says, *"How GOD anointed Jesus of Nazareth with the Holy Ghost and with power:* **<u>who went about doing good, and healing all that were oppressed of the devil; for GOD was with him.</u>"**

Armed with this truth, I went out and started praying for the sick everywhere. Many people were healed of back problems. I prayed for a woman and she received cartilage back in her knee; people with severe headaches received healing. One of my favorites was praying for a man in AutoZone who was having a hard time walking and was bent over with a cane. I asked him if I could pray for him; he said yes. I prayed a simple prayer, less than ten seconds, and then I walked away. The store clerk was watching me with a look of awe on his face. He told me to turn around; as I turned around the man's back straightened up and he walked out of the store with his cane in hand. All this time, fasting and praying for hours to create the atmosphere for GOD to heal, not knowing that the atmosphere, "the anointing" was already within me. We cannot create or produce more anointing; it is only activated by faith. The measure you are seeking is already in you!

But **the anointing that you received from him abides in you,** *and you have no need that anyone should teach you. But as his anointing teaches you about everything, and is true, and is no lie—just as it has taught you, abide in him.* (1 John 2:27)

WHY DO YE MARVEL?

It is GOD's goodness that draws a man to repent. Ministry is representing GOD in the earth and manifesting His kingdom through signs, healing, deliverance, casting out demons, teaching, and acts of love. What I love about Jesus is what he said after the 70 returned excited because of the miracles they did. In Luke 10:20 he says, "Marvel not, do not rejoice that spirits are subject to you, but rejoice that your names are written in heaven."

Why would Jesus say, "Marvel not?" The disciples, I think, were sharing with their leader the excitement of the miracles performed. Can you imagine the journey back to Jesus? Pure excitement, joy, and hugs as they walked back to Jesus. I imagine them talking over each other because their joy cannot be contained. They saw Jesus do miracles; now it was their turn. Have you ever been so excited to tell someone something only to be turned off when they were not as enthused as you? This was that moment. Joy quickly turned to, "Huh—what? Jesus I only did what you told me to do?"

Of course, we rejoice when GOD does something amazing, but this was not that. I believe Jesus was setting protocol. Is it possible to experience success in ministry and be lifted in pride, which is why Jesus mentioned Satan's fall? Never take GOD's glory. Stay humble at all cost because your ministry depends on it.

You may be thinking, "I am not qualified for GOD to use

me." Well, even Judas Iscariot was given authority in Luke 9:1 to cast out demons and cure diseases—so why can't God use you also? You are qualified right now to do the same acts of Jesus, who by the way paid for it all.

I want you to excel in ministry, not for a position, accolades, or clout, but rather to excel in the spirit of love. Let GOD cultivate your character, using the trials, tribulations, stress, affliction, and the fire of life to prove you. If you allow GOD to nurture you, it will give you longevity in ministry. Dr. Munroe said it best, "Talent without character is like a shooting star. It shines bright for a moment then it's gone. In contrast, character is like the sun, it shines consistently and is reliable."

CHAPTER 5

THE CALL OF LEADERSHIP

-Lead for God's Sake!

"To most effectively lead others, love others. Genuine love moves powerfully and impacts more deeply than any title or position of authority" - Todd Gongwer

The purpose of being sidelined is all about leadership. GOD wants to establish great leadership in your life, but what kind of a leader will you be? Will you be the leader who cuts corners seeking instant gratification?

49

Will you be the leader who is discourteous and arrogant? Will you be the leader who delegates work, but is not the first one to pick up the hammer? Will you be the leader who is unable to accept criticism? Will you be the leader who demands perfection, but does not demand it first within? Will you be the leader who embraces change? Leadership demands character and integrity. Character is who you are when no one is watching. Integrity is what you do when no one is watching. How will you lead?

How Will You Lead?

Luke 16:11 (ESV) says, *"If then you have not been faithful in the unrighteous wealth, who will entrust to you the true riches?"*

The question presented in Luke 16:11 is: Can you, who is unable to manage earthly wealth, be trusted with the riches of GOD? The Bible says true riches. What are the true riches? True riches are people. Should you, who cannot manage earthly possessions, be trusted with people?

Being a leader is the highest honor one can attain. Leadership comes in all forms: a father is a leader, a mother is a leader, and even a child can lead. Leadership does not mean you need a pulpit or an audience. Leadership does not need a congregation or a choir to sing *amen*. Leaders are defined by who they influence. And great leaders make decisions for the benefit of everyone and not themselves. I do not care how great your talent or skill is, if you have a history of making selfish decisions then you are not ready to lead at this moment. Sit on the sidelines until you learn.

The goal or the endgame of any great leader is to put oneself out of being needed. The responsibility of a leader is igniting the hidden leader within the individuals they lead. If you pastor a church, you should be able to walk away and the church never misses a beat. If you are a business owner, you should be able to step away and the business still operates without your presence.

Take, for example, a business owner and an employee. Both are leaders. Both contribute to the culture and growth of the company. The employee plays a key part by promoting the culture and influencing peers. The owner is accountable for driving the culture and is tasked with managing under the spotlight. The difference is in the duties, but the leadership model is the same.

HOW WILL YOU MANAGE UNDER THE SPOTLIGHT?

I often joke around with many different pastors, and I say that if you want to know if a pastor is a good leader ask their spouse. If you want to know if a mother or father are good parents, ask their kids. The individuals we lead are the fruits of our leadership. They tell the story of how we lead. If any leader is displeased with the environment they see in the workplace, at home, or in their church, just know what is seen is a reflection of the shadow they cast while leading.

The condition of our nation, whether good or bad, falls on leadership. Nothing disgusts me more than seeing a leader place fault on the individuals under their leadership. The role of the leader is to take the fault, acknowledge it, own it, develop action items, and steer the ship in the right direction.

It is especially important to know the ideology of the leader because that is how they will lead. How we lead is a direct result of the philosophy we believe. Decision-making flows out of the belief system. What you believe and how you behave will determine how you will lead. When it comes to selecting a pastor, manager, CEO, or political candidate, please do not be deceived by charisma. Do your research: look at previous behaviors and decisions that were made. This will give a snippet of the philosophy of the leader and how they will lead. If we are not vigilant, we will be deceived, and corrupt leaders will be put in the seat of authority that will drive racism, poverty, confusion, and disparity.

Leadership is the heartbeat of the father. He said He calls pastors (leaders) after His own heart. Many believers can teach, preach, minister, and evangelize, but a pastor is chosen solely on their heart.

> *"And I will give you shepherds after my own heart, who will feed you with knowledge and understanding."*
> Jeremiah 3:15

THE SHADOW YOU CAST

I first heard Senn Delaney's term "the shadow of the leader" (also referred to as shadow of influence) during a culture training at my job. The facilitator asked everyone the question: "What shadow do you cast?" She went on to say that people pay attention to what we do, more than to what we say. And as a leader your shadow can either build people up or tear them down.

The shadow you cast as a leader is the outward manifestation of glory. Glory in its simplest form means the full weight or nature of a thing. Your ideology, attitude, behavior, and beliefs make the physiology of your shadow. The shadow of the leader is what people say about you when you are not present. That's the shadow! It is the residue of your character that is left in the room. That character residue will either inspire creativity and ignite the hidden leader within or create an environment that is counterproductive to growth.

With that perspective, think of Peter's shadow. Acts 5 says that people even carried out the sick into the streets and laid them on cots and mats, and that as Peter came by, they hoped to receive a miracle by the power of "his shadow." The Bible does not record anyone healed by Peter's shadow, but his shadow became a point of contact and people released their faith. His shadow inspired hope for the hopeless!

The shadow loses its power when your character is considered disreputable by those you lead. I challenge every leader to let your shadow shine bright!

The Grace of a Leader

A great leader can lose it all by saying the wrong thing. It could happen by sending the wrong tweet, snapchat, or Facebook post. Having grace as a leader is knowing when to speak and how to speak; understanding who you are speaking to and the tone and delivery of the message. A much-needed conversation can be ineffective if the tone is not sincere and is laced with sarcasm and venom.

How you talk to the people you lead is critical. Here are a few conversation tips to help you.

- Always look them in the eye when you are speaking.
- Look them in the eye when they are speaking.
- Let them finish what they are expressing before interrupting.
- You are not listening, if while they are talking you are thinking of an answer.
- Make sure the tone of your voice is low.
- Take ownership.
- Look for a solution.
- Ask them how you can support them.
- Have empathy.

As a leader you must hold yourself accountable for you how show up to a conversation. If you show up with a bad attitude, then do not be surprised if the conversation yields no results. I encourage you to show up with a curious mindset, willing to learn something in the conversation that you did not know before. When you show up like that, you open the door for **admittance** *(openness)* and **reconciliation** *(understanding or resolution)*.

Long-suffering is having grace. In my leadership training classes, I was told that as a pastor I need to develop a duck neck. Just like water pouring down a duck's neck is the same way I need to be with people, meaning I do not attack every situation. I analyze the individual and give mercy for uneducated behavior. As a leader it is important to know the people you lead and what issues to address. Leadership in the 21st century has no place for passive-aggressive leaders. I repeat: The 21st century has no place for passive-aggressive leaders.

Leadership is knowing the difference between someone who is struggling versus someone who does not want help. I tell the story about the pig and the little lamb. If you put the pig in the mud, the pig will wallow in the mud, play in the mud, and splash in the mud, because the pig loves the mud. If you put a little lamb in the mud, the little lamb will cry out, looking to be rescued. The significance of the story is that the pig represents one person and the little lamb represents another; the mud is a representation of indiscretion. Both individuals are in the mud; one does not want help, but the other does. Be careful because you think you are judging the pig when really, it's the lamb you are judging. <u>It takes grace to know the difference.</u>

The Courage to Say It

Simple and to the point! Do you have the courage to say, "I am sorry?" Do you have the courage as a leader to say "I am sorry?" People often want to know if they are growing in maturity and I ask them one simple question: Are you able to say sorry after you made a mistake? If you can say "sorry" that is a step in the right direction of maturity.

Some leaders may find this complicated, but remember you are tasked with driving the culture of your ministry, business, and home.

> *"When I was a child, I talked like a child, I thought like a child, I reasoned like a child. When I became a man, I put the ways of childhood behind me."*
> 1 Corinthians 13 (NIV)

The Watchful Eye

King David's life was leadership. His journey from childhood to king is a witness to us all. David was a mighty man of valor with integrity and fear of the LORD. What I admire about David is he never sought leadership, yet people followed him. Amazing! David was anointed to be king, yet he was sidelined for character building. GOD called him and eventually, David would rule but his teacher by the name of T. I. M. E. had other plans. It was fifteen to twenty years between the time when David was anointed until he was king.

David Had Grace

Can you imagine having someone you look up to as a mentor, only to have them turn their back on you? That's what happened to David. Saul was supposed to be David's mentor. A mentor is someone who helps develop you on your journey. A mentor provides sound wisdom, counseling structure, and encouragement. But what happens when the mentor becomes jealous of the mentee? Saul tried to kill David on many occasions. Yet, in the midst of being hunted by Saul, David never wavered in grace. David had many opportunities to kill Saul but he gave him grace.

As a leader, grace is when you have the power to punish but give mercy. Demonstrating grace to the individuals you lead keeps the door open for self-development. If you want to have open and honest communication with those under your leadership, build them up more than you critique them.

Minister to Your Emotions

A good leader can sabotage their ministry, team, and business if their emotions are not in check. As leaders we cannot allow our emotions or the emotions of those we lead to neutralize the vision. Something I learned a long time ago from my Bishop was that people will be people. And they will do things to make you question why you are in ministry with them and probably why you hired them. However, a leader should not lash out in anger by slamming doors, yelling, cussing, and sighing. Yes, a sigh is dangerous. Take Moses, for example. GOD commanded him to speak to the rock in Numbers 20. There was no water in the community and the people gathered in opposition to Moses. They complained and asked Moses, "Why did you bring us out of Egypt to this terrible place?" They blamed him, so Moses went to GOD for instructions. GOD told him to speak to the rock so the people could witness the power of GOD. Instead, Moses was agitated by those under his leadership, so he addressed the crowd by saying, "Listen, you rebels" and he struck the rock twice. He disobeyed GOD and allowed his reactions to damage his leadership.

However, in a desert hill country named Ziklag, we examine a different story. In 1 Samuel chapter 30, David and his mighty men arrive back in Ziklag and discover it was burned. Raiders from an enemy camp took David's wives and his men's wives and carried them away. The Bible says when David and his men saw the city ransacked and torched they cried out and wept aloud until they could weep no more. That is agony at the deepest level. Their agony was so deep that they talked about stoning David. He was a man who they trusted with their lives, now they wanted to kill him. Between losing his family to raiders and his men desiring to kill him, David was racked with pain. He felt intense emotions from his men and within himself. But this is the moment! When your back is against the wall, what is in you will be brought forth. And what was in David was a heart for the people. He did not lash back; instead under extreme stress he stood on his principles and consulted a higher power.

What good is a leader who does
not carry a pocket mirror?

SIDELINED

Being sidelined does not mean you stop working or serving and move into a cave waiting for your character to develop. NO! Sideline means you keep working, serving diligently in ministry. And when your character has been cultivated, GOD will expand your influence.

*"His master said to him, 'Well done, good and faithful servant. **You have been faithful over a little; I will set you over much**. Enter into the joy of your master.'"*
Matthew 25:21

Can You Handle Being Sidelined?

To my Launch Team, thank you!

Bobby Rauch, Brandie Adair, Marcus Timmons, Montel Timmons, Denise Lovelady, Diana Burkhalter, Amanda Mae, Louis Metcalf, Terry Williams, Lakeisha Williams, Fonda Martinez, Ryan Moyle, Jeff Bratz